WHAT HAPPENS WHEN

Someone I love doesn't feel good

SARA OLSHER

-WITH- JENNI ROGERS, MS, CCLS, C゙

Hi! My name is Mia!

And this is **Stuart.**

Stuart is very curious, and sometimes he gets a little worried
when he doesn't understand something.

Stuart wants to know ... **how do our bodies work?**
And **why do some people's bodies get sick and not get better?**

Bodies are really, really **COOL!** They are made up of all kinds of different parts that make us think, and move, and feel.

OUTSIDE THE BODY

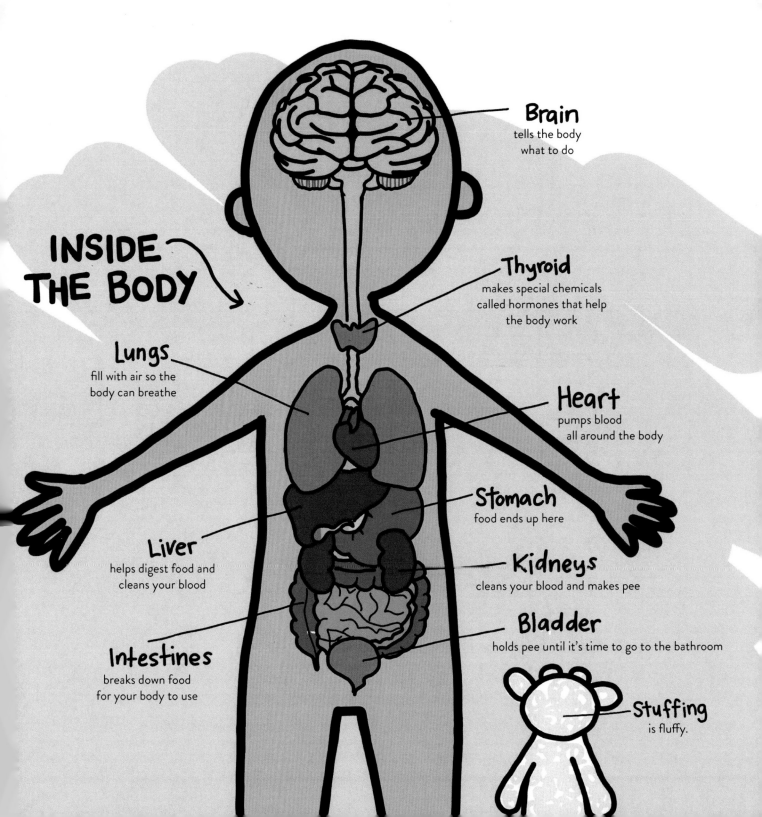

INSIDE THE BODY

Brain
tells the body
what to do

Thyroid
makes special chemicals
called hormones that help
the body work

Lungs
fill with air so the
body can breathe

Heart
pumps blood
all around the body

Liver
helps digest food and
cleans your blood

Stomach
food ends up here

Kidneys
cleans your blood and makes pee

Bladder
holds pee until it's time to go to the bathroom

Intestines
breaks down food
for your body to use

Stuffing
is fluffy.

You might already know this,
but our bodies, like every living thing,
are made up of tiny little things called cells.

Cells are like blocks, but they put *themselves* together.

One really cool thing about cells
is that one cell can turn itself into two cells
anytime it wants.

(Whoa, right?)

That means cells can build and build and build.

It's like building with LEGO® and never running out of blocks!

imagine the tower you could build!

Every cell has a job.
Together these cells build body parts,
and then tell them how to work.

Cells make hearts pump, legs walk,
lungs breathe, and so much more!

We are cells! We are sooo tiny, you can't even see us. But we are what bodies are made of.

We are blood cells!

Hi! We are skin cells!

And we are heart cells!

Cells make it so bodies can do everything they need to do to be alive.
They turn food into energy, make poop and pee out of food and water
we don't need, and keep all the body parts healthy.

The mind is thinking, the person is feeling,
and all the most important body parts are doing their jobs.

When you think about it,
it's pretty amazing that our bodies
make all this stuff
and *do* all this stuff
without us having to think about it!

Most of the time, our bodies do everything they need to do.
But sometimes, things aren't working quite right.

There are a few ways that cells
might stop doing their jobs
the way they should.

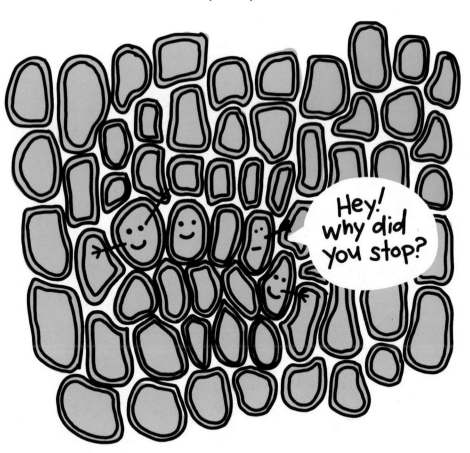

Sometimes cells accidentally start making broken cells.

These cells can crowd out the cells that are trying to do their jobs by taking up lots of space or getting in the way.

Usually, the body can get rid of broken cells before they start crowding the other cells.

But sometimes too many broken cells are made, making it hard for healthy cells to do their jobs.

Other times the cells get confused,
and instead of getting rid of broken cells,
they get rid of cells that are doing their jobs!
And then no one is left to do that job.

Not all cells are builders.
Some cells help
the body
in other
ways.

We need
them all!

If the cells can't do their jobs well,
the body part they build or help won't work right —
which is not good when we want the body to stay alive and feel good!

When that starts to happen,
we go to the doctor to help the body parts work better.

If the lungs aren't working right, the body might get the oxygen it needs from a big tank.

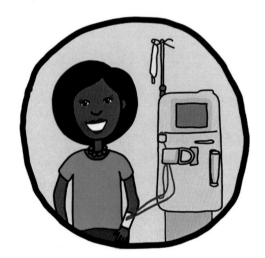

If the kidneys aren't working right, the body might have its blood cleaned a different way, using a machine.

Doctors might try to remove broken cells using surgery or medicine.

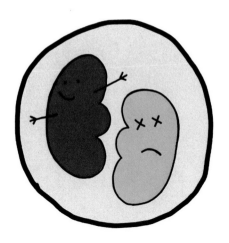

Or, they might use another body's healthy cells (or healthy body parts!) to help the body heal.

They might use medicine to help certain cells work better.

Doctors can do some pretty cool stuff!

Some bodies get tired more easily than other bodies.
Sometimes they need a cane, or a wheelchair, or a nap every day.

But even with help, sometimes the body is
just too tired to do what everyone wants it to do.

When we have a long list of things we want to do,
and the body is only able to do a few of them,
that can be frustrating for everyone.

When you want to do something fun
and the person's body isn't able to do it,
it is normal to be disappointed, or angry, or sad.

It's not fair!

...but we had a plan!

Saturday's Plan
1. Waffle breakfast
2. Swimming
3. Park picnic & tag
4. Laser tag
5. Homemade pizza
6. Friends sleep over!
7. movie night

When that happens, we have to feel our feelings,
and then make a new plan.

You and your grown-up can put both ideas on a calendar.
This will help you to know what to expect each day.

It's normal to feel **LOTS** of feelings about this.
Sometimes we have one emotion at a time,
and other times we have a whole bunch of emotions
at the same time, and it can be confusing.

Like sadness.

Loneliness.

Anger.

This happens to both kids and grown-ups.

BIG emotions can make us feel terrible.

Emotions live in our bodies and in our brains.

The good news is that there's lots of ways to calm your body and brain down, including...

Our bodies and brains might need different things at different times.

Taking a walk might help
one time, but not the next.

That's why we need to learn a bunch
of different strategies.

drink water

jumping jacks

take a walk

read

cuddle time

Play with play doh or slime

sea salt bath

color or draw

deep breaths

blow a pinwheel

tapping

play music

blow bubbles

be with an animal

Sometimes you might have a hard day.
When that happens, you can tell your grown-up,
"I am having a hard day. Are you having a hard day too?"

...and think about how you can get through
those big feelings together.

Maybe you need to cry together for awhile, and then make a plan:
Do we need to watch a movie?
Do we need to walk around the block?
Do we need to color for a little while?
How do we make the next five minutes better?

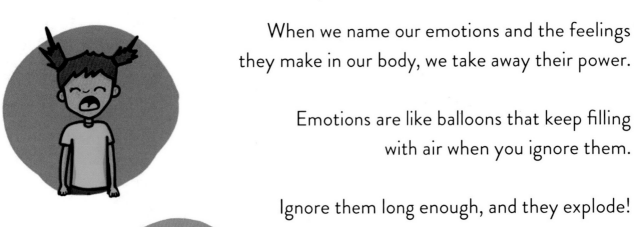

When we name our emotions and the feelings they make in our body, we take away their power.

Emotions are like balloons that keep filling with air when you ignore them.

Ignore them long enough, and they explode!

When we name our emotions and let ourselves feel the feelings in our body, they take about 90 seconds to float away.

Feelings can also explode when we don't talk about them.

We might get stomachaches or headaches, not because we're sick,
but because we're holding in our feelings.

That's why sharing is important.

Because the more we keep our feelings inside, the bigger they get.

Sometimes it is hard to say our feelings in words, because they are just **TOO BIG**.

It helps us to draw
or write them out,
or play songs for each feeling.

When a whole family is feeling **big** feelings,
the grown-ups are feeling it too.

Sometimes grown-ups don't tell kids about their feelings.
They want you to know that it's their job to take care of their own feelings
AND help you with yours.

Sometimes they don't ask you about your feelings.
They might think asking makes it harder for you.

And maybe you don't share your feelings with them
because you worry about making your grown-up sad.

But talking about it **ALWAYS** makes it better.

It makes us feel less alone.

And there are **lots** of grown-ups who care and want to help.

Sometimes things are hard, and we wish they were different.
But Stuart feels better now that he knows what to expect
and how to help himself feel better.
And don't forget...

Hi! My name is Sara. Nice to meet you!

I wrote this book (& lots of others!) because I like to draw + help people.

reading

Dancing (Badly)

my family

Things Sara LOVES!

animals

nature

Quiet time

CRUNCHY ICE!

Rainbows

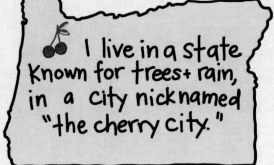

I live in a state known for trees + rain, in a city nicknamed "the cherry city."

I live with my daughter and our three cats, Tater Tot, Waffle, and Batman. One day, I want a **goat**, and a want to name it CAULIFLOWER!

 I do all my drawings on an iPad with an Apple pencil

And my name is Jenni. I help kids when someone they love has a big illness.

I live in the "Grand Canyon" State. Like Sara, I live in my state's capital city.

trees

my family

sweets

Things Jenni LOVES!

Singing (badly) in the car

military jets

I work at a famous hospital called Mayo Clinic*

*The views expressed are the author's personal views, and do not necessarily reflect the policy or position of Mayo Clinic

Hey Parents!

Let's be real: talking about
a chronic or terminal illness is HARD.

As a cancer survivor myself, I've been there.

Get this PDF guide for free
at mightyandbright.com/illness

Mighty + Bright's CCLS-approved guide for talking to
kids will help reduce stress and anxiety for the whole family.

You'll learn how to:
- explain your specific illness;
- connect with your ;
- encourage open communication;
- introduce the topic of death;
- help them cope ongoing.

SCAN THIS USING YOUR PHONE
or visit: mightyandbright.com/illness

Book Sara for school visits and
public speaking at saraolsher.com

mighty + bright™

Published by Mighty + Bright
mightyandbright.com

ISBN: 979-8-9867765-3-8

want to tell
Sara something?
Send a letter!

Sara Olsher
13203 SE 172ND Ave
Suite 166, #1121
Happy Valley, Oregon
97086

Made in United States
North Haven, CT
23 March 2024